FRESHWATER AND MARINE BIOMES

Knowing the Difference

Science Book for Kids 9-12
Children's Science & Nature Books

BABY PROFESSOR
EDUCATION KIDS

Speedy Publishing LLC
40 E. Main St. #1156
Newark, DE 19711
www.speedypublishing.com
Copyright 2017

The two major water or aquatic biomes are the freshwater biome and the marine biome. In this book, you will be learning about the characteristics of each of these biomes so that you will be able to tell one from the other.

THE MARINE BIOME

The marine biome mostly consists of saltwater oceans. It covers about 70% of the surface of the Earth and is the largest biome on the planet.

DIFFERENT TYPES OF MARINE BIOMES

While the marine biome mostly consists of the saltwater oceans, it can be separated into three different types:

OCEANS: The five predominant oceans covering the world include the Pacific, Atlantic, Artic, Southern and Indian Oceans.

Pacific Ocean

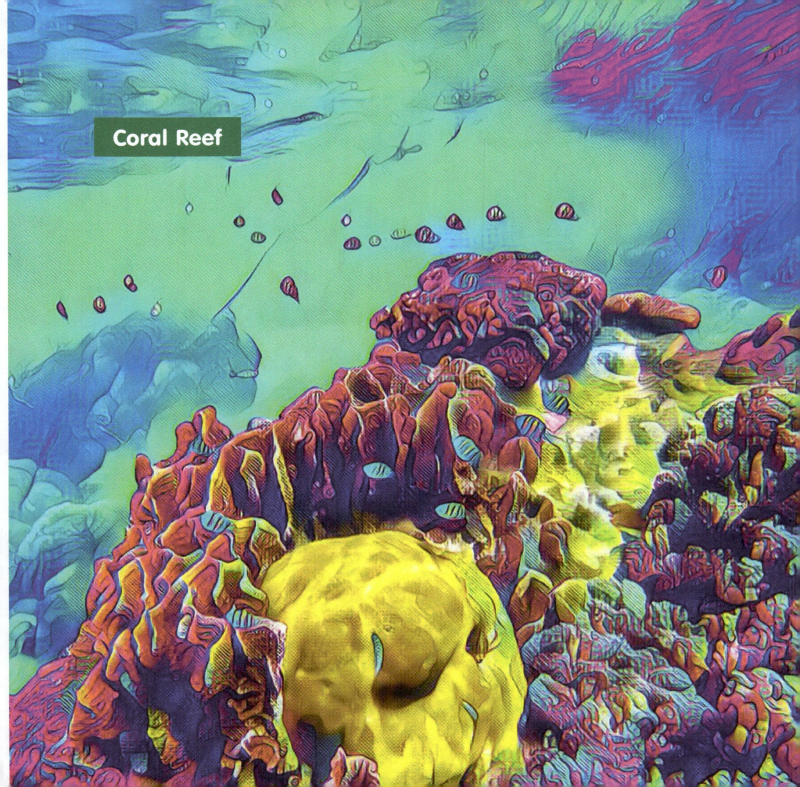

Coral Reef

CORAL REEFS: When they are compared to the oceans, they are relatively small, but approximately 25% of marine species live in these reefs and therefore make the coral reefs a vital biome.

ESTUARIES: The areas where the streams and rivers flow in the ocean are known as Estuaries. This is where saltwater and freshwater meet, creating a biome or ecosystem of its own including diverse and interesting animal and plant life.

Estuary

OCEAN LIGHT LAYERS (ZONES)

The ocean is separated into three zones (layers). These are referred to as light zones since they are based on the amount of sunlight that each zone receives.

The sunlit (euphotic zone) is the layer at the top of the ocean which receives the most sunlight. Its depth can vary, but averages approximately 600 feet deep. The sunlight gives energy to the organisms in the ocean by photosynthesis. It also feeds plants and tiny organisms known as plankton. The plankton are quite important since they provide the basis for food for a lot of the remaining ocean life. Consequently, about 90% of life in the oceans lives in this zone.

Artemia Plankton

Bioluminescent Creature

The Twilight (disphotic zone) is the zone in the middle of the ocean. This area is about 600 feet to about 3,000 feet deep, dependent upon how murky it is. There is not enough sunlight to sustain plant life in this zone. The animals that live in this zone have been able to adapt to surviving without much light. Through a chemical reaction known as bioluminescence, some animals are able to create their own light.

The Twilight (disphotic) zone is the zone

The Midnight (aphotic) zone is the layer below 3,000 or so. There is no light and it is totally dark. It is quite cold and the pressure of the water is very high. There are only a few animals that are able to adapt to living in these extreme conditions, living off of the bacteria that gets energy from the cracks in the Earth located at the ocean's bottom. Approximately 90% of the oceans falls into this zone.

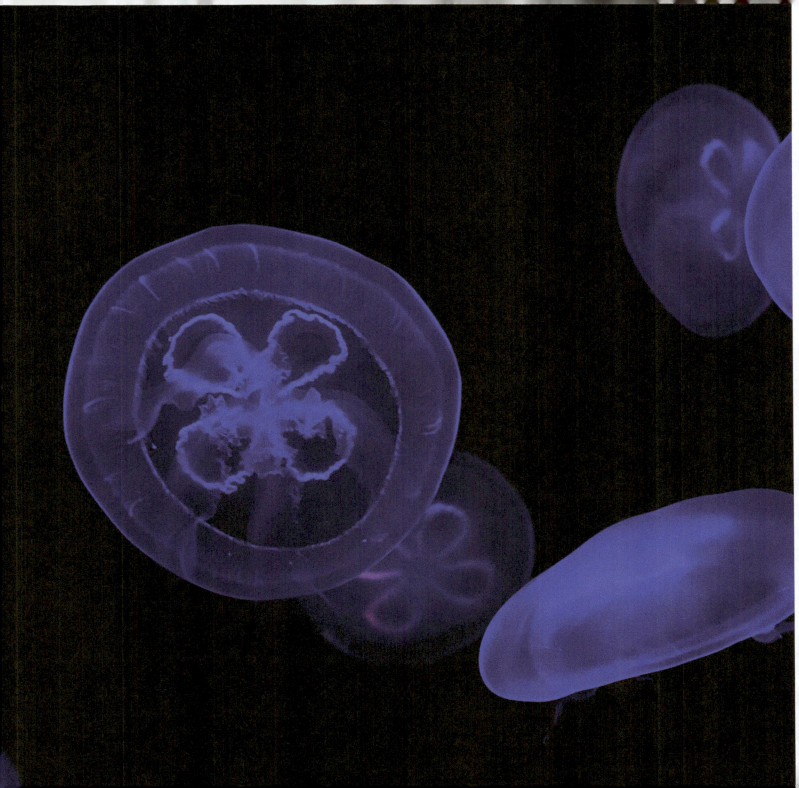

Octopus

MARINE BIOME ANIMALS

The marine biome consists of the most biodiversity of all of the biomes. A lot of the animals, including fish, have gills allowing them the ability to breathe water. There are other animals, known as mammals, that have to come to the ocean surface to breathe air, but still spend much of their lives in the water. The mollusk, another type of marine animals, is made of a soft body that does not have a backbone.

Here are some of the animals that call the marine biome home:

FISH – Includes swordfish, sharks, clown fish, tuna, stingray, grouper, eels, flatfish, seahorse, rockfish, gars and sunfish mola.

MARINE mammals – Includes seals, blue whales, walruses, manatees, otters and dolphins.

MOLLUSKS – Includes cuttlefish, octopus, clams, squids, conch, oysters, snails and slugs.

Fishes

Seaweeds

MARINE BIOME PLANTS

There are thousands of plant species living in the ocean, and they depend on photosynthesis for energy from the sun. Plants living in the ocean are vital to all life on Earth. Algae absorbs carbon dioxide and supplies much of Earth's oxygen. Some types of algae include phytoplankton and kelp. Other types of plants in the ocean are mangroves, seaweeds and sea grasses.

FRESHWATER

The definition of the freshwater biome is having a lower salt content compared to the marine biome which, as we learned earlier, is comprised of saltwater.

Underwater in Freshwater

Freshwater Lake

TYPES OF FRESHWATER BIOMES

Freshwater biomes consist mainly of lakes, ponds, streams, rivers and wetlands.

LAKES AND PONDS

Lakes and ponds are often referred to as lentic ecosystem. They have standing or still waters, they do not flow like streams and rivers. Some of the larger lakes around the world are the Caspian Sea, The Great Lakes, Lake Baikal, Lake Tanganyika, Lake Titicaca and Lake Victoria.

Lake Baikal

Littoral Zone

Lakes are usually separated into four biotic community zones:

➲ The littoral zone is the area that is close to the shore and were aquatic plants like to grow.

Como lake

- The limnetic zone is the open water surface of the lake, which is away from shore.

- The Euphotic zone is below the water's surface where there is enough light for the photosynthesis process.

- The benthic zone is the bottom, or floor, of the lake.

A lake's temperature can vary over time. The lakes will stay the same temperature in tropical areas, and the water will get colder the deeper you go into the lake, which gets less sunlight. In northern areas, the lakes change in temperature as the seasons change.

Lake Tahoe

Lake animals include crayfish, plankton, snails, frogs, worms, turtles, fishes and insects. Lake plants include cattail, water lilies, bulrush, duckweed, bladderwort and stonewort.

STREAMS AND RIVERS

These are often referred to as lotic ecosystems, meaning that the water flows, not like the still waters of lakes and ponds. Their size can vary dramatically from a small trickling stream to rivers that are a mile wide and go for thousands of miles.

Stream

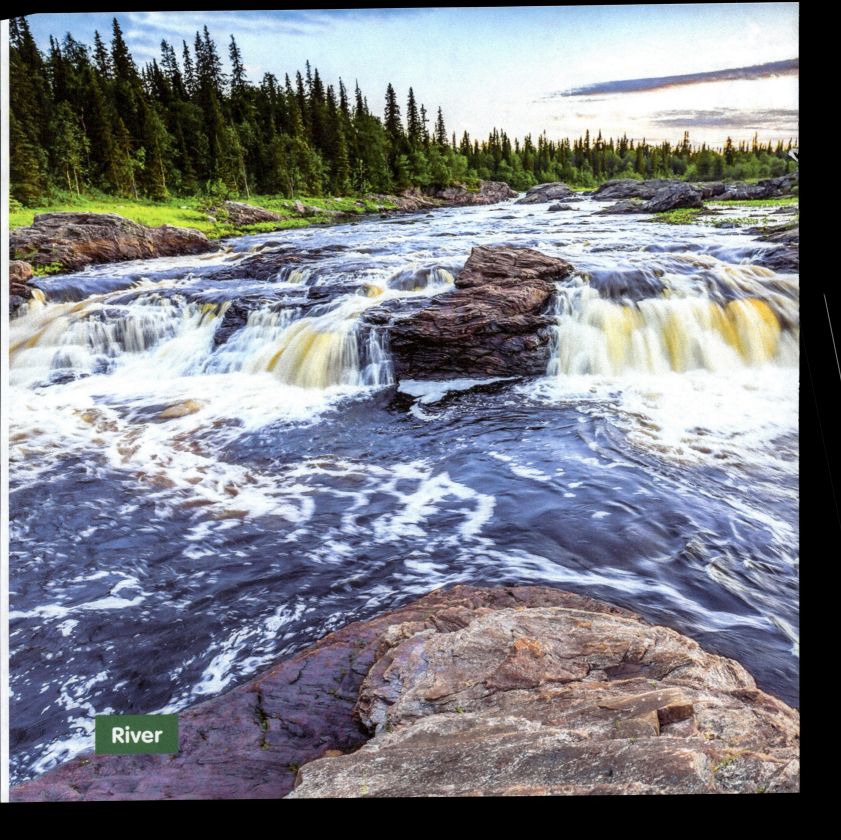

River

The water for a river can come from melting snow, rain, ponds, lakes and even glaciers. Most people believe that rivers always flow to the south, however, 4 out of the 10 longest rivers around the world flow to the north.

The ten longest rivers of the world are the Nile, the Amazon, the Yangtze, the Mississippi (Missouri), the Yenisei, the Yellow, the Ob, the Irtysh, the Congo, the Amur and the Lena.

River Nile

The following are the key factors that influence the ecology of the rivers and streams:

FLOW is the amount of water as well as the strength at which it flows, impacting the types of animals and plants that are able to live in a river.

LIGHT provides energy for the plants using photosynthesis. The amount of light resulting from the change of seasons or possible other factors will have an impact on a river's ecosystem.

THE TEMPERATURE (CLIMATE) of the land which the river is flowing through has an impact on local animal and plant life.

CHEMISTRY involves the type of geology through which the river is flowing and will have an impact on what type of rocks, nutrients, and soil are in the river.

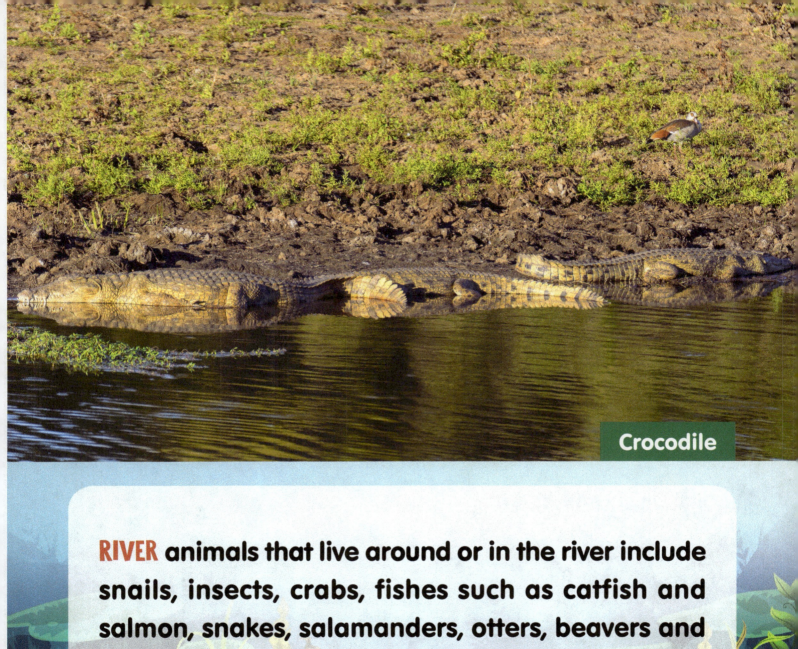

Crocodile

RIVER animals that live around or in the river include snails, insects, crabs, fishes such as catfish and salmon, snakes, salamanders, otters, beavers and crocodiles.

Birch

RIVER plants growing around the rivers will vary quite a bit dependent upon where the river is located. Typically, plants will live along the river's edge where the water is flowing at a slower pace. Plants include river birch, tapegrass, water stargrass, and willow trees.

WETLANDS BIOME

The wetlands biome combines water and land. Another way to think of it is land that is saturated with water. It may be mostly underwater for a portion of a year, or flooded only at certain times. One key characteristic of a wetland is that it sustains aquatic plants.

Depending on where the wetland is located, the amount of rainfall can vary quite a bit. It might be over a hundred inches in a year or as little as seven inches in a year.

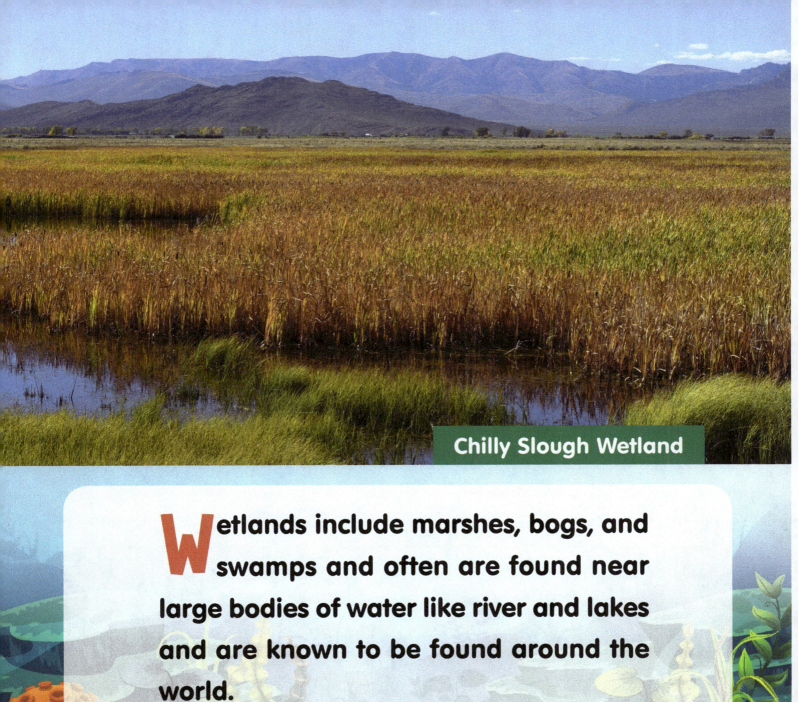

Chilly Slough Wetland

Wetlands include marshes, bogs, and swamps and often are found near large bodies of water like river and lakes and are known to be found around the world.

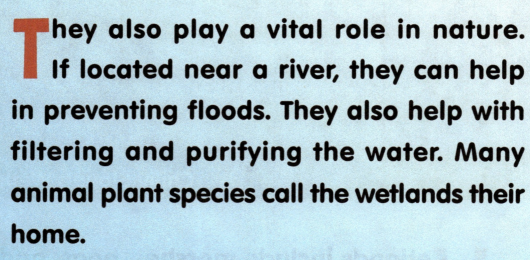

They also play a vital role in nature. If located near a river, they can help in preventing floods. They also help with filtering and purifying the water. Many animal plant species call the wetlands their home.

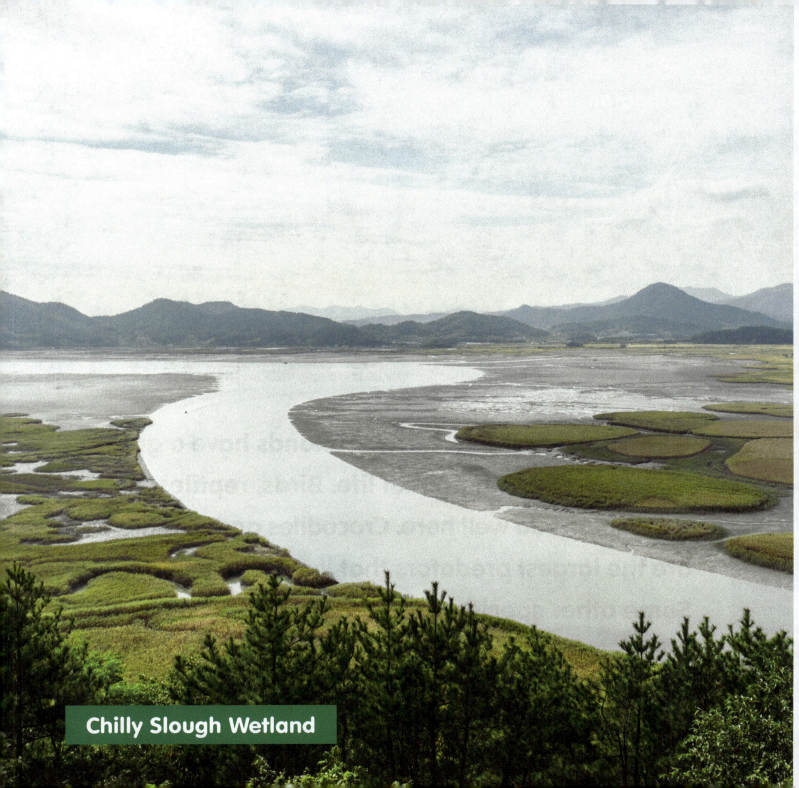

Chilly Slough Wetland

Alligator

Wetland Animals -- The Wetlands have a great diversity with animal life. Birds, reptiles, and amphibians do well here. Crocodiles and alligators are the largest predators that live in the wetlands. Some other species of animals that live here are minks, beavers, raccoons, deer and minks.

Water Lilies

Wetland plants – Plants are able to entirely grow underwater or float on top of it. Other plants, like large trees, mostly grow outside of water. These plants include water lilies, mildewed, duckweed, cattail, mangroves and cypress trees. The world's largest wetland is the Pantanal, located in South America.

Now that you have learned about the differences between Marine Biomes and Freshwater Biomes, you may have questions about another biome, the Coral Reef Biome. For additional information, you can go to your local library, research the internet, and ask questions of your teachers, family and friends.

Visit

BABY PROFESSOR
EDUCATION KIDS

www.BabyProfessorBooks.com

to download Free Baby Professor eBooks
and view our catalog of new and exciting
Children's Books

Printed in the USA
CPSIA information can be obtained
at www.ICGtesting.com
LVHW081647170923
758459LV00042B/498

9 781541 914247